# CHAUN VAUGHN

# Being *Heart* Forward

## An Others Centered Leadership Guide and Workbook

Copyright © 2016 Chaun Vaughn

All rights reserved.

ISBN-13:978-1537772585
ISBN-10:1537772589

This book is dedicated to my mom, Gwendolyn Anderson, who is my inspiration for leading a heart forward lifestyle. She is truly an others-centered individual and I strive daily to be more like her.

Love you mom

# TABLE OF CONTENTS

|  | About the Author | i |
|---|---|---|
|  | Acknowledgements | ii |
|  | Introduction | 1 |
| Chapter 1 | **Being Heart Forward- The Meaning** | 2 |
| Chapter 2 | **Principle 1: Transparency** | 8 |
| Chapter 3 | **Principle 2: Awareness** | 15 |
| Chapter 4 | **Principle 3: Accountability** | 24 |
| Chapter 5 | **Principle 4: Others Centered** | 32 |
| Chapter 6 | **The Beginning of a Heart Led Society** | 40 |
| BONUS | **Leadership Productivity Hacks** | 44 |

**CHAUN VAUGHN** is a wife and a mom first and foremost, but she has a strong desire to create change in the workplace, in her community and in the world.

Chaun Vaughn is a dynamic speaker and trainer helping to take individuals and businesses alike to a higher level. She brings humor and enthusiasm to every speaking engagement and enjoys working with companies to build a motivated team.

She specializes in Leadership, Team Building, Customer Service, and Generational Differences and has wowed many. It was only natural that she would write a book on her take on leadership.

## ACKNOWLEDGMENTS

I would like to thank my husband, Derrick Vaughn, for his continued love and support.

A big thank you to my son, Isaiah.
You are why I work as hard as I do.

Thank you to each and every one who encouraged me along my book writing journey. I am truly grateful for each of you. You know who you are.

# Introduction

Because I truly want you to get the most out of this quick read, you have to come in with an open mind and I desire for learning something that you may not be used to.

You can read this book quickly and really underestimate what has been shared. So, I encourage you to reread and read again to get the full picture of what I am really trying to convey.

This is not a leadership book for the traditional leader. This book is designed for the leader who wants to lead outside the box, take risks and develop future leaders. If you are not willing to see if change is needed in your leadership style, then you may need another book.

Change in the workplace, in our homes, in our communities will always begin with you.

Here's to changing the world through leadership,

# BEING HEART FORWARD
## THE MEANING

# BEING HEART FORWARD

You have attained one of the most important goals you have set for yourself. You are now a **LEADER**. You could not be more excited about your new leadership role. You have the skills and you know you have prepared to be the best leader….EVER! Then you take a pause….. and you ask yourself, *"Why would anyone want to follow me?"* Sure, your skill set for the position is stellar, but you have to wonder, *"am I truly a leader?"*

When I moved into my first leadership role, this is definitely a question I asked myself. I had the degree, I made sure I worked hard to prove that I was the best choice for the job, but the evening before I took on this new role, I realized, my skills alone were not going to make me a leader others would want to follow.

Anxiety set in. I worked hard to excel in every opportunity and this was no different. Failure was not an option in my new position. Now, I am not only responsible for my success, but the success of others as well. I realized, it's no longer just about me and my goals or dreams, but now I have a group of people who also have goals and dreams and who will look to me to help them accomplish those goals.

I have to admit, I started to show some selfish tendencies. "If I did it on my own, they can do it too." Then it hit me. I did not get to where I am by myself. It was not only Chaun Vaughn who played a part in my success. I paused and thought, I will be a good leader! But how? Will my new team trust me? Will they confide in me or will I be the boss they talk about behind my back? I mean, let's be real, we've all had that boss who was so driven by their own personal ambition that they treated their employees any old way and neglected their needs just to ensure that they were meeting their own personal objectives and goals. I sat there and thought, I don't want to be THAT boss! So what was I going to do?

I went into my memory bank and I thought about all the leaders I have come across. The leaders I admired as well as those who, well, left a bad taste. I then wondered, why did I admire certain leaders? What was it about them that stood out? The answer that kept coming to the front of my mind was how they displayed care and trust. They had a genuine concern for those they were leading. *They led with their heart*.

As I extended my thought process on this, I focused on exactly what the leader did to make me admire them and how they did it. This is when I created a simple, but very effective formula to follow.

This process, if you want to call it that, consisted of factors that I innately possessed and some that, well frankly, I needed time to improve on. So, I made a decision that night to be the leader who I admired. The leader whom I did not mind following. I chose to be a **HEART FORWARD** leader.

## Being Heart Forward

What is being a Heart Forward leader, you may ask? Before I answer that question, we must first understand the true meaning of a leader.

Below are a list of words. Circle each word that you feel relates to a "leader".

Task Oriented      Results Driven      Controlling      Transactional

Inspirational      People Driven      Vision      Charismatic

Honesty      Reactive      Followers      Subordinates

## Did you choose these words?

Inspirational, Honesty, People Driven, Vision, Followers, Charismatic,

If so, then you have a pretty good idea of who and what a leader is.

A leader has a **vision** and the determination to see that vision through. A leader uses his or her **charisma** to get others to buy in to their vision and assist with accomplishing it. A leader is NOT defined by a title. Many people in management feel that if they have the title they are automatically a leader. This cannot be further from the truth. Anyone can be a leader, from the CEO of a Fortune 500 to a frontline worker. If someone is willing to follow you, then you, my friend, are a leader. Being a leader is all about **building relationships.** So, back to the initial question.

## What is being a *heart forward* leader?

Well, simply put, you are leading with your heart. Your leadership is focused on those you are leading. It's who you are at your core. It is recognizing that there is more than you in this big world. Bringing it down to an even smaller scale, it is knowing that there is more than just you, the leader, on your job who aspires to accomplish things. It's realizing you need those you are leading just as much as they need you.

In this book, we will focus on developing a Heart Forward attitude, consistently. You will be guided through four principles. You may already possess a few of them, but there may be a couple you may need improvement in.

## *"Treat others the way they want to be treated"*

As we move through this leadership guide and workbook, the platinum rule is great to keep in the front of your mind, **"treat others the way they want to be treated"**. It sounds simple and it can be as long as you see its meaning as taking care of your staff the way they expect. This and only this will yield the results you expect. It's no secret, you will work harder for someone who has your best interest at heart. As the old saying goes, "you catch more bees with honey".

Write in your own words what being heart forward means to you.

_____

_____

_____

_____

_____

# BEING HEART FORWARD

## PRINCIPLE 1
## TRANSPARENCY

## BEING HEART FORWARD MEANS BEING TRANSPARENT

I have always felt that I was not the best at making friends. I'm not sure why that is. Even though I appear to be an extrovert, I secretly believe I am very shy and introverted. So making friends has always been quite difficult for me.

I do have some awesome friends that I have made throughout the years. When I think about how we became close and remained close, one simple word comes to mind. I, we, were **transparent**.

Letting that covering of shyness or even pride down and allowing them to see the real me, who I am, is what I attribute to our long lasting friendship. My friends know they can confide in me, trust in me and believe in me because they are comfortable with me and vice versa. This can be said within a work environment as well. Heart Forward leaders are transparent.

As a leader it is important to let your staff know who you are. I mean really let them know *Who You Are*. Knowing who you work for and what they stand for speaks volumes. I have never been comfortable with someone unless I felt I knew a little about them, their character, and their background. When I knew nothing about a leader, I always felt our work relationship to be questionable.

*Should I share this? Should I not? Am I asking too many questions? Am I not asking enough questions? Should I consult my leader because I'm struggling with this project or will that make me seem incompetent?*

That can make for a very stressful work environment. I would have never made life-long friends if I had not been transparent. At the same token, I will never have a cohesive, trusting staff if I do not allow them to see who I am.

**Transparency Session**
As I stated, I am not naturally an open and transparent individual, so I knew that being transparent with my team would be a hard task for me to accomplish. I decided during my first meeting with my staff that I would give them the opportunity to come up with questions about what they wanted to know about me, personally and professionally. They could come up with these questions individually or as a collective group. I assured them I would answer all their questions at our next staff meeting.

Knowing that I had just opened myself up completely, I was terrified! How personal will they get? Will they ask questions out of curiosity or to tear me down? Nevertheless, I agreed to do this and I was going to stand behind my word.

I knew this process was a great start and had the potential to work because I experienced this first hand with a leader I had.

When she hired me, part of my orientation was to come up with personal and job-related questions solely about her. We sat there in my orientation and she answered every question I had. I asked about her family and where she was from (because her last name was one I had never heard). I asked about her flaws, what she is doing or has done to improve her flaws, what were her strengths and was she open to possibly learning from me. Although awkward for me, I know it had to be very difficult for her as well. However, through this process I learned so much about her and she inadvertently learned quite a bit about me. This was powerful to me and I held on to it, even after I left that position.

That conversation was so impactful and she was definitely a leader I truly admired. I felt as though I knew her, I trusted her and I knew she cared about me and my goals. I even felt comfortable speaking with her and getting her opinion on applying for a position outside of the company a few years later. If we had not developed the relationship in the beginning, I would never have felt comfortable enough to share my aspirations for another job with her. I probably would have applied for the position and submitted my two-week notice. That was something I just could not do. I valued her and her opinion meant a lot to me. To this day, I still value her opinions. Anytime I am faced with a difficult decision when it comes to work, I reach out to her. She has since retired, but is still a valuable person and source of advice in my life all due to her transparency.

## Expectations

The staff meeting was a success. I answered the questions and I could instantly see they were a lot more at ease with me than the days prior. I knew they were trying to figure me out. Once the transparency session ended, we were all a little more relaxed with each other. It was then I shared my expectations.

*A Heart Forward leader knows that being transparent also means laying out your expectations.*

In order for the transparency conversation to be beneficial, as a leader you have to set clear and concise expectations for the team up front. Let them know that your main goal is to see them succeed and that you value their feedback. You are there to assist them by being a servant leader, but there are expectations.

## Benefits

Being transparent has many benefits for "true" leaders. Through transparency, you are a REAL person in the eyes of your team. This means that you are authentically cultivating and growing relationships. This makes team building seamless. A team that trusts their leader works smarter and more efficiently, therefore, accomplishing tasks quicker. Going back to those questions I mentioned earlier, 'Should I share this? Should I not? Am I asking too many questions? Am I not asking enough questions? Should I consult my leader because

I'm struggling with this project or will that make me seem incompetent?' With transparency, these questions are no longer an issue because the team is no longer fearful of sharing their opinions nor fearful about discussing where they may be weak.

Transparency is truly the key to becoming a leader others want to follow. It removes the ego we may possess and provides balance between what we know and who we are. Transparency in leadership is simply letting your staff know you are human.

Is being transparent easy? Certainly not, which is why there are many businesses that still suffer from high turnover. Being transparent takes work and does not happen overnight. Becoming transparent takes time, but there are some practical ways to work towards being more transparent.

1) Acknowledging staff as you enter. A simple greeting goes a long way. Have you ever had THAT boss that would walk in, look at you and not speak a word? The atmosphere for the day is set and moral has dropped.

2) During staff meetings share something fun you did over the weekend or a family win. A great way for people to learn who you are, is through how you interact with your family.

3) Engage with your team as often as you can and recognize them for their efforts

4) By all means share any knowledge you are privy to regarding the company. Staff members like to know what's going on in the workplace. They are there to help promote the mission. The office is not a place for surprises.

If after reading this you feel transparency is a trait you need to work on, do not put it off. Your success in leadership depends on your transparency.

How will you become transparent? List five (5) ways below on how you can become a more transparent leader and then put them in to practice.

1. _____

2. _____

3. _____

4. _____

5. _____

# BEING HEART FORWARD

## PRINCIPLE 2
## AWARENESS

# BEING HEART FORWARD MEANS BEING AWARE

Growing up, we all heard it. Anytime we were away from our parents or going somewhere with friends, we heard, "be aware of your surroundings". We either took this to heart or blew it off. In my mind, I always felt that I was "aware" of my surroundings. I just knew, that in the event something would or could arise, I would be ready, because I had already assessed the situation. I felt prepared to act because I was aware.

These days, it means so much more to me since I have a child of my own. When I am out shopping with him or if we are at the park, I am always on high alert, looking around to make sure everything is as it should be because now I am responsible for not only myself, but for this precious life that was gifted to me. This new found awareness comes from my genuine love and care for my son to be all right while we are away from the comfort of our home.

You may be wondering, what does this awareness have to do with leadership? Well, I would say that is a great question.

Being placed in a leadership role is just like having your own child. It's a special gift. And with any special gift, you will love and care for it and look out for it. As a leader, those who are following you are your gift. So you should always want what's best for them. You should be aware of what each brings to the collective.

**Awareness in Action**

Take a look around while at work. What do you see? What stands out? Is there an employee who is always complaining but does a wonderful job? Do you wonder why? Is there someone who helps to keep the team motivated? What do you see?

Jot down three (3) things that stand out to you.

1. _____

2. _____

3. _____

Keeping an observant eye out for wins and even fails, I feel, is a practice that should be common among great leaders. This will keep you in touch with what's going on within your team. The potential of the team is great, we just have to be open-minded to see it.

Go back to the items you listed above. Now take the time to create dialogue that will foster effective communication regarding those observations. Use this as the perfect opportunity to encourage your staff by sharing your observations regarding each of them personally and professionally. This is where having a keen sense of awareness comes in to play and where truly being a servant leader should shine through. If an employee is doing a stellar job with a project, share that with them. If an employee is not performing up to your expectations, let them know, but always communicate on a level, whether the situation is good or bad, that promotes their aspirations and how that aligns with the company's goals. Many times as leaders, we feel that the best time to discuss issues with employees is during their employee evaluation, but reaching out more frequently fosters positive communication and positive attitudes and it helps keep you, the leader, in the know.

> **"You will never know the potential of your staff if your focus is only on self"**

Make it a point to truly see, hear and know what is going on within your company, within your team. Your employees want and need to hear how they are doing and how they are contributing to the sustainability of the company. You will never know the potential of your staff if your focus is ONLY on self.

**Self-Awareness**

Along with being aware of what is going on with your staff, it's also wise to be self-aware. To be self-aware means that you have taken an assessment, an authentic, realistic assessment of your abilities and who you are as a leader and as a person.

A common request when on an interview is to share your strengths and weaknesses. Most of the time we can get right in to what our strengths are but sometimes struggle with our weaknesses. Why is that? Have we been programmed to feel that being in a leadership position means we MUST know everything ALL the time and if we show that we don't know it all, then what we are actually capable of doing is now in question? Being self-aware is definitely the opposite of that. There are always areas within our job and even our life where we are not excelling. I mean, we can't get it right all the time. Owning up to that can be difficult, but know this, regardless if we choose not to acknowledge our flaws and weaknesses, our staff and others see them.

Admitting when you don't have the answer does not make you a failure, but it does make you better because now you know there is an area where you can be better. What is golden about being self-aware is when you are truthful and honest about your strengths and more so your weaknesses, your staff respects that honesty. In their eyes you are trustworthy and credible.

**Strength vs. Weakness Exercise**

Take 30 seconds and list all your strengths. Take another 30 seconds and list your weaknesses.

| Strengths | Weaknesses |
|---|---|
|  |  |

How easy was it for you to list your strengths? Was it just as easy to list your weaknesses? My guess is no. We are more in tune with the areas we excel in but less aware of the areas that need improving. Most of the time we refuse to acknowledge our weaknesses because frankly, we can get caught up in our weakness and throw ourselves a pity party. We must learn to use our weaknesses as a motivation tool to improve certain areas of our professional and personal life. It is important to note where we may need improvement because it is only then we will be able to pour in to our team effectively.

**Activity**

Take our above weakness and prioritize them based on the weakness that would affect you most to the least. This will give you the order in which you should focus on them. Now, complete the action plan below for each weakness.

**List highest priority weakness**

_____

**What is your plan of action within the next 30 to improve?**

_____

_____

_____

_____

**What is your plan of action within the next 60 days to improve?**

_____

_____

_____

_____

**What is your plan of action within the next 90 days to improve?**

_____

_____

_____

_____

**How will you evaluate your progress?**

_____

_____

_____

_____

**Will you have an accountability partner?** _____

If yes, list their name and be sure to include them in your action plan.

_____

Use this process to complete an action plan for each weakness listed.

# PRINCIPLE 3
# ACCOUNTABILITY

## BEING HEART FORWARD MEANS BEING ACCOUNTABLE

The term "accountable" alone can make anyone nervous. In leadership, accountability means you take ownership of the good and the bad that happens within your team. That can be scary because in leadership we always want to appear to be on top of everything. When a plan or expectation is not met, owning up to that failure, in our eyes, gives the image that we are incompetent and cannot perform our job. This is far from the truth. I always say, "Growth and success are born from failure". Learning from our mistakes and our team mistakes, only gives us ammunition to fire off something spectacular. As a leader, taking accountability also further elevates our trust-worthiness with our team.

*Growth and Success are born from failure*

**Owning Failure**
Being a leader is not always glitz and glam. There are many challenging days, hours even minutes. Wouldn't it be great to say everyday your team got it just right? My guess is, although as leaders, we put forth a ton of effort in our team, ensuring they truly understand their duties and the final goal doesn't always materialize as we hope. What makes this even harder,

is that, as a leader, the end result is ultimately **our responsibility**. Yes, we are held accountable for when our team has not performed as they should have.

This is by no means the time to start with the blame game, which, unfortunately is so easy to do. Blaming your team for the failure of a project or task could lead to low morale and distrust, which is exactly what you do not want to happen. This, instead, is the exact time to ACCEPT responsibility and **TAKE ACTION**. This is the very moment a Heart Forward leader can prove his or herself. A heart forward leader will evaluate what was done well as well as evaluate what needs improving and communicate take that with the team.

I like to use my parenting as examples when trying to fully understand being and performing as a Heart Forward leader. My son struggles a little in math and this new math truly boggles my mind. He was preparing to take a math test. I gave him my instructions and goals. I told him, 1) he must study every day, 2) practice with the worksheets I found (from the internet, ha!) and 3) do your best on the test and bring home an A. He studied, he asked for the worksheets to practice with and he brought home a C. My first thought was to blame him for not studying well and not doing all that he could have done to make a better grade. All I was doing was blaming him for his failure to bring home that A. Boy was I wrong in doing that. What this led to was my son feeling like he was no good in math and probably wouldn't be because he DID study and he DID utilize the study aids I provided for him. Where did I go wrong? I failed to see that there were many opportunities for me to make sure he fully understood what he was studying. Maybe, I didn't step in as I should have because I failed to recognize that the new math truly intimidated me. In this situation, I should have made myself more available to assist in his studying and then owned up to the fact that I feared tackling this new math myself. I had to look at me to see where I needed to improve to make sure he would improve by the next test. I had to accept responsibility for him not doing as well as he could have because I simply gave instructions and removed myself from the process of studying with him due to my own fear.

I needed to make this right. I researched the various math problems he was bringing home so that I could help him complete and work through the math worksheets. I inserted myself into his study time, quizzing him and ensuring that he truly understood each concept. We were learning together. What do you think happened on his next test? He brought home that A.

If I had not evaluated my part in this situation and only focused on the negative end result, the C, my son would always feel defeated when it came to math. When you truly want someone or your team in this case, to excel, even after a failure, you should always ask, what can I do to turn this failure into success.

Has your team fallen short of a goal? What was your response to this outcome? Did you evaluate how you contributed to the outcome? Is there something you could have done differently to change the outcome?

These are questions you must always ask yourself when your team has not performed as you had hoped. Sharing with your staff on how you could have helped them better achieve the goal, positions you as a more humble and trustworthy leader. You now have a team that will work harder for you because you stayed away from the blame game and accepted responsibility for the part you played.

**Activity**

**Reflect on a project that your team worked on but did not complete to your satisfaction. Write that incident down.**

_____
_____
_____
_____
_____
_____
_____

Now, answer each question, honestly.

**How did you respond to your team when this project or goal did not yield the results you?**

_____
_____
_____
_____
_____

**How did you contribute to this project? To your team?**

_____
_____
_____
_____
_____
_____
_____

**What could you have done better as the leader in this situation?**

_____
_____
_____
_____
_____
_____
_____

### Heart-Forward Praise

Let's journey back to the story of my son and his math grade. As a parent I was very excited that he made an A on that next test. He was excited as well. He worked hard to turn that grade around. So when he shared his excellent grade, I praised him for his accomplishment. Did I play a part in making sure that he was ready to take that test? Yes, however, as a heart-forward leader we must learn to be accountable for when our team has not performed as planned but give praise when they reach the expected outcome.

Sounds unfair? Not to the heart forward leader. You are responsible for the not so good results but your team should always receive the praise for the good, even when you had a hand in helping them obtain that goal. Take my son for instance, how would he have felt if I had said to him, "You know you made that A because I gave you the tools and helped you study? You know you wouldn't have done that well without me, right?" Can you imagine what he would be thinking? Feeling? He would have felt defeated, his morale would have been lowered and now that A wouldn't seem as wonderful as it first did. Why? Because now I am taking the credit for his hard work.

Being a Heart-Forward leader means truly wanting to see your team excel and when they do, praise them for their hard work. This in no way diminishes what you have done and contributed, but in turn builds your team up to make your job even easier because they now know that you genuinely want to see them do their best. When your team does well, you in turn do well and that doesn't go unnoticed.

Have you praised your team for accomplishing a task or goal?

## Constructive Feedback

It is wise to note that along with praise, constructive feedback is also necessary. Yes, the team has excelled and attained the goal set in place, but a leader must also share feedback on what could have been done differently to make the process more efficient. Being heart forward does not mean you overlook the issues of the team, but you share the areas where each could improve. Again, this must be communicated in a way that lets the team know you are supporting their growth professionally. Keep in mind, praise is a method used to build confidence and motivate the team whereas constructive feedback is used to correct potential problems and grow the team.

# PRINCIPLE 4
# OTHERS CENTERED

## BEING HEART FORWARD MEANS BEING OTHERS CENTERED

The title of this book is *Being Heart Forward: An Others Centered Leadership Guide*. Each area we have touched on plays a part in being others centered, but now it is time to discuss exactly what that means.

Why will your team follow you? What will motivate them to give their all for you and the company?

Believe it or not, it all depends on who you are, and the character you display. YOU are why others will follow you. Leaders are relationship builders and in order to build relationships, you have to have genuine concern for those of whom you are building a relationship with.

Being others centered is not the easiest task, mainly because our entire life has been all about us. So we are always going to look at how a situation will affect us before we look at how it has an impact on someone else.

The time is now! It's time to learn how to view life through the eyes of others and put "me" in the background.

> ***Each of you should look not only to your own interests, but also to the interests of others.***
> ~Philippians 2:4

**Servant Leadership**

I have referenced being a servant leader a few times throughout this learning journey. Did you question what servant leadership is? A servant leader truly wants to serve the team first. This is a leader who puts the needs of others ahead of their own and helps to develop the team. This is a leader who is not caught up on the title of being a leader, but focused on the fact that everyone on the team has value to add and deserves to be acknowledged and respected for their contributions. Some leaders are naturally servant leaders, it's who they are. For others, including myself, it requires hard work and dedication. I'm not saying that I'm not a good person, but sometimes I can be a selfish person. It is normal.

So how do I work towards being others centered? There are people around you who possess this trait and you must insert yourself in to their world. Watching how they interact with others daily and use what you observe as a teachable moment. When you are surrounded by others who are servant leaders, you begin to think how they think. It will soon become second nature.

Traditional leadership focused solely on the person as a leader. I call this the *selfish leader*. This type of leader ask questions like,

> *What are my goals? How will I accomplish them?*
>
> *What will I get for attaining my goals?*

Every thought and move depends on what they want and not what benefits the team. When you lead with this mindset, you alienate your team and reaching those personal goals you are so focused on may not be as simple as anticipated, because believe it or not, you need your team. Contrary to the selfish leader, a servant leader possesses a selfless attitude. Instead of questioning, what are my goals, the question becomes what are the goals of the team as it relates to the mission and vision of the company? Instead of, how will I accomplish my goals, the question becomes, how can I help the team reach their goals? This is the thought process of a true others centered leader. This leader knows that when you do all that you can to ensure your team excels, you too excel as the leader.

**Actively Listen**

Are you a great listener? Do you actively listen to your team? Active listening may sound easy enough, but how many times has someone come to you and you miss half of the conversation because you have either formulated an answer or because you had something more important (you feel) on your mind? When you are actively listening, you are giving your undivided attention to the speaker. You are listening so intently that you could repeat everything they have spoken. This shows that you have shifted your focus from you to them. Being an active listener has its perks. You are in a great position to learn something you may not know either related to work or something personal about the speaker.

**How to become a better listener**

1) Listen intently and give the speaker your undivided attention

2) Use body language to show your engagement in the conversation

3) Never judge. Let the speaker convey exactly what they are expressing without interruption

4) Provide feedback only when prompted or signaled

Active listening conveys to the speaker that you respect what they are sharing which further boosts their trust and confidence in you as a leader.

**Take the Quiz**

Are you "others" centered or "self" centered?

| | | |
|---|---|---|
| When interrupted by an employee while involved in completing a task at my desk, I am able to stop and actively listen | T | F |
| I am more happy when I focus on others before myself | T | F |
| This week I have looked for ways in which I can help my team members succeed | T | F |
| I praised a staff member this week | T | F |
| I have volunteered within the past month | T | F |
| When I win, my team wins | T | F |
| My words are in alignment with my actions | T | F |
| I make sure that whatever my team needs to accomplish a task, I provide it | T | F |
| I am receptive to feedback and learn from it | T | F |
| I help team members prepare for their next level within the company | T | F |

If you answered TRUE to all, you are a true model of an "others"-centered leader. But, every great leader knows that there is always room for improvement.

If you answered TRUE to six or more, you are a leader who is concerned about the team, but you may have a few areas that you need to focus on to ensure you are leading with others in mind.

If you answered TRUE to five or less, you have some work to do when it comes to being an others centered leader. There is nothing wrong with this, but in order to develop a team that will trust and respect you and do all that they can for you, this is a trait you will want to work on.

Look at the statements you answered FALSE to. Analyze why you chose false. Let's get to the root of the issue. Once you have written down your why, brainstorm ways the false can shift into a truth.

Becoming an others centered leader means overcoming any fears you may have that put you in a place of dominance. Yes, fears are what lead to pride and a domineering persona because we are trying to hide our insecurities. Becoming a servant leader means constantly asking yourself, 'why am I doing this? Who am I doing this for?' You know that you are truly becoming that heart forward leader when you can honestly say, I am doing this because I have the means to help others succeed and that's who I am doing this for......others.

***The more you help others succeed, the more you will be positioned as a leader others want to follow.***

Do not feel as though you do not play a part in the equation when you focus on others, because believe me, you do. You will soon see how putting others before you will elevate you to heights you could have never imagined. Your success is the byproduct of your servant leadership. The more you help others succeed, the more you will be positioned as a leader others want to follow.

## THE BEGINNING OF A HEART-LED SOCIETY

## The Beginning of a Heart-Led Society

Being Heart Forward is a process that may be easy for some and more difficult for others, but it is definitely attainable. Recognizing that in order for your team to flourish, you as their fearless leader must truly want them to succeed and you must unequivocally want to do whatever you can to help them succeed. This heart forward philosophy is based on a leader having a selfless, others centered viewpoint. It's allowing yourself to be transparent with your team so that they feel a sense of comfortability and trustworthiness with you as their leader.

### *The word of the day is SUCCESS*

As a leader, we strive for *SUCCESS*. Everyone wants to be successful! What does success look like for you? Is it moving ahead while pushing others down? It can be pretty lonely at the top. Or, is it moving ahead while helping others progress as well?

Success is a word that is used loosely. Most believe that success is measured by how much money you have or the "things" you possess. This could not be further from the truth. True success happens when you help others realize their potential for success and assist them in getting there. When we maximize our true potential, not only for self, but for the benefit of others, then and only then have we attained true success.

This leads to a feeling of accomplishment and self-worth. This is your contribution to society. This is your contribution to the team.

Being successful doesn't mean having all the stuff, but it means touching others along your journey while being a leader.

It's time to make a difference in the workplace, in the community, in the world. It all begins with being Transparent, Aware, Accountable and Others Centered. Can you imagine an atmosphere where everyone is focused on performing at their best because they trust and respect their leader? When this happens, you have become a success!

**The Challenge**

I challenge you, yes you, the person reading this book, to put into practice leading in a heart forward way, daily. You must be consistent and you must truly want to create change. It's in you or you would have never chose this book to read. The workplace needs more leaders like you. More leaders who start the conversation for change. Remember, **True Leaders are Visionaries! True Leaders Inspire! True Leaders are Others Centered!**

## True Leaders are Heart Forward.

# Being Heart Forward is the *KEY* to *SUCCESS!*

# BONUS

## Leadership Productivity Hacks

Being a heart forward leader will take time and as leaders, we may forget to focus on being heart forward because our time cam become scarce throughout the day. This is when being productive counts. Listed below, as an added bonus are 20 productivity hacks that help keep me focused. If you have productivity tips, please share with me on any of my social media platforms. That information is listed at the end of this book.

## 1. Take Advantage of Your Mornings and Your Nights

It is no secret that when you wake up in the morning you are full of energy. Your mind is alert and you know that you can accomplish and tackle anything that comes your way. Use this to your advantage! Early in the morning work on those tasks that will require more creativity or deep thinking, because your brain is ready for it.

We all know that as the day progresses, we become lethargic and we start thinking of those things we have to do once we leave work. You're not as productive at this time. So this is the perfect time for more simple tasks, tasks that don't require much effort.

For some reason at night, just before bed, my brain cranks up again. Use this as your opportunity to write down any ideas that may come to mind and this makes it easy to refer back to them when needed.

## 2. Know Your Time's Worth

Focus only on what you can do and if someone on your team is capable of completing a task, then you need to DELEGATE. When we, as leaders, try to do everything ourselves we can become burnt out and if we are overworking ourselves, we cannot be a productive, heart forward leader. Utilize your team and value your time.
Set time aside just to clear your mind, relax and refocus.

## 3. Block Out Distractions

There are so many ways we can become distracted during the day, which will kill productivity. We have phone calls and Facebook notifications, emails and all these things that prevent us from completing a task or goal during the day. Set a specific time frame for each goal or task for the day and work uninterrupted for that particular time. You may need to put your phone in airplane mode or close out of your email program, but do what you need to do to block out your distractions. I like to work for 45 minutes straight and then take a 10-15 minute break and repeat. I will quickly check emails or Facebook during that break, but when that time is up, I'm back to being productive. I get so much accomplished during that time.

## 4. Standardize Your Sleep

Getting a good night rest makes all the difference in being productive. If your sleeping habits are random, your days will be too. Always plan to get at minimum 7 hours of sleep a night. You will then wake up refreshed, alert and ready to lead!

## 5. Exercise

To prepare your body to be productive you must exercise. When you exercise, your blood starts flowing and your brain is more active, which will create a more productive day.

## 6. It's Ok to Say NO!

It is ok to want to help all the time. I have a term for this, "chronic pleaser". That's me, no doubt, but trying to please everyone eats away at needed time for my goals and visions. Learn to say no and know, it's ok.

## 7. Take Back Those Commute Hours

If you are not fortunate to work from home or very close to home, commuting to and from work can eat up a lot of time. Take those commute hours back! Instead of scheduling phone meetings during the day, schedule them for your commute home.

## 8. Create a Happy Desk

When my desk is covered in paper and sticky notes and pens, etc., my stress level will soar. It looks as though nothing is getting done and I am not being productive, when actuality, I just have a lot of unnecessary items that either need to be filed or thrown away. Declutter your desk daily so that when you arrive to work each morning, you start fresh and stress free.

## 9. Be a Breakfast Champion

Kids hear it all the time. Eat your breakfast. It's the most important meal of the day. Well, newsflash! Breakfast is not just for kids. Eating a healthy breakfast each morning plays a major role in being prepared to be productive. Breakfast jumpstarts your body, otherwise you will be hungry very early in the day and therefore will become unproductive. You can really be a champion when you eat breakfast.

## 10. Set Goals. Realistically!

Goals are meant to be, wait for it……ATTAINABLE. Nothing is more of a productivity killer than working toward a goal that literally cannot be reached. Set realistic, time friendly goals and watch your productivity soar.

## 11. Be Heart Forward with Your Team

Being Heart Forward will not only create a productive team, but will create a productive you.

## 12. Experience the Outside during the Work Day

In the office literally all day? That's enough to make anyone stir crazy. To come out of an unproductive slump, step outside and take in God's beautiful creation

## 13. Reserve One Day a Week For…..

Reserve one day a week for a no schedule day. Don't schedule anything! Use this as a catch up day, an email responding day, a whatever it needs to be day.

## 14. Keep Like Company

You've heard the old saying, "Birds of a feather flock together". Well, keep people in your circle who are productivity pros. You can always learn from each other.

## 15. Prepare for Monday, Friday

How many times has Sunday come and you have gone in to a panic about what is to come on Monday. Change that! Start preparing for Monday on Friday and keep your Sunday panic and stress free.

## 16. Be On Time

There's not really much to say here. When you're on time, you get things done.

## 17. Be Early to Rise

As a follow up to hack #16, wake up early. This is a hard one for me, but I do seem to get more accomplished when I wake even just 30 minutes earlier. It's easy to be on time.

## 18. Create an Organized Computer Desktop

I have a co-worker who has hundreds of documents and excel spreadsheets and folders on his desktop. It makes me stressed just looking at it. I feel more productive when my desktop home screen is organized and not cluttered. Just like your desk, keeping your filing system more streamlined can create productivity.

## 19. Carry an Attitude of Positivity All Day

Positivity breeds positivity, so as a leader if you remain positive, then your team will remain positive. When your team is positive, then you are not having to refocus them.

## 20. Unplug and Refocus on the Weekend

Self-explanatory!

# NOTES

# NOTES

# NOTES

# NOTES

Let Chaun Vaughn know how you are doing on your journey to Being a Heart Forward Leader by sharing your progress with her. You can reach out to her on her various social media platforms.

   facebook.com/ChaunVaughnSpeaks

   instagram.com/ChaunVaughnSpeaks

www.ingramcontent.com/pod-product-compliance
Lightning Source LLC
Chambersburg PA
CBHW070402190526
45169CB00003B/1075